J. TERRY JOHNSON

ESSENTIAL THOUGHTS
FOR WINNERS

*Life Lessons from
the Golf Course*

Foreword by
LOREN ROBERTS

10

ESSENTIAL THOUGHTS
FOR WINNERS

Editing by Barry Lyons
Cover and Interior design by Kandi Evans

Published in the United States of America

ISBN:978-0-9884051-6-5

1. Self Help
2. Sports

9.15.21

DEDICATION

This book is dedicated to my colleagues who are members of the Men's and Women's Golf Associations at Horseshoe Bay. Martha and I enjoy their company on the golf courses and at local social events. They inspire us to play better golf and to be better competitors. We consider them *winners*, one and all.

A special salute is extended to the Wednesday Summit Rock group, led by my friend Cully Exsted. Patient, friendly, reassuring, and so much fun on the golf course. Thanks, Cully, for serving as the "commissioner" for our band of duffers.

Acknowledgments

The narratives for some books flow easily, from conceptual ideas to final drafts. Others lumber along, failing to find traction, and require a push to get them over the finish line. *10 Essential Thoughts for Winners* would fall into the latter camp. After writing a chapter or two, I pushed the pause button, allowing other creative writing to move into the forefront. That was at least three or four years ago.

Had it not been for the coronavirus debacle of 2020, *Winners* might still be in limbo. Needing projects to provide daily structure for my monotonous life during weeks of "social distancing," I discovered the initial chapters of an abandoned manuscript, buried with other unfinished writings in my computer's documents file. A quick read-through of the anecdotes convinced me to move forward with the book. The vibes were good. One year later, here it is!

Speaking of structure for long days of isolation, golf has become a lifesaver for Martha and me during the pandemic. The golf courses at Horseshoe Bay remained open, even during the height of the COVID-19 scare. Reading, writing, telephone calls, Zoom meetings, television binge-watching, and countless rounds of golf became the daily features for our survival regimen. My handicap on the golf course did not go down, but I developed a new appreciation for the restorative benefits of the game.

Hats off to friendship. A serendipity from playing golf is the blessing of making friends. Martha and I have made new acquaintances when teeing up the little white ball and we have strengthened the ties with old friends as well. As in any setting where we meet new people, some merely pass through our space, while others command a seat at the table. We cherish the friendship of all, wishing them well on the links and in their respective lives.

Reagan Lambert is deserving of special mention. Having recently retired after more than thirty years serving as director for the Fellowship of Christian

Athletes in the greater Austin area, Reagan has become an honorable servant leader in the Horseshoe Bay community. He likes people; moreover, he likes to help people. And, by the way, he carries a single-digit handicap on the golf course.

Knowing that *Winners* needed a boost from someone who might be willing to write the book's foreword, Reagan said, "I know just the right person for that task. Loren Roberts!" In a matter of days, Reagan contacted his friend, secured his commitment to write the foreword, and delivered a draft that was ready for publication.

Loren Roberts is a winner! Having competed at the biggest venues of professional golf, he knows what it takes to win. Over his career, he has won eight PGA Tour tournaments, thirteen PGA Tour Champions events, and two European Senior Tour events. He has also been recognized by his peers as being one of golf's true gentlemen, on and off the course. Thank you, Loren Roberts, for accepting Reagan's request to write the foreword to my book and thank you Reagan for carrying the water on my behalf.

Finally, a book without editing, layout, cover design, and quality-controlled printing is just a manuscript waiting to be discovered. I am grateful for the team that assisted me with the many details involved in publishing *Winners*. Barry Lyons edited the copy. Kandi Evans designed the cover and arranged the internal layout. Shelly Sapyta and her team at Baker-Taylor Publishing Services produced the final product. I am indebted to them for their professional skills and personal encouragement.

CONTENTS

FOREWORD

Lessons learned on the golf course have often been compared to the more important lessons we learn in life. Passion, patience, perseverance, and preparation are all essential elements to a good golf game.

As a professional, I have had the opportunity to play some of the most fabulous golf courses in the world. Each venue has offered a unique experience, featuring spectacular vistas and a scorecard full of challenging holes. It has been a privilege to have played on world-renowned, championship courses as well as an assortment of municipals tucked away on the back roads to nowhere.

I encourage you to take the time to read *10 Essential Thoughts for Winners* by J. Terry Johnson. Using ten fabled golf courses from Hawaii to Wisconsin as a backdrop, Johnson has recounted the experiences of golfers, some professional and others less notable, to illustrate life lessons originating from the game. You will relate to these stories. They are your stories too. At the end of each chapter, you will likely be able to add a tale or two of your own.

Finally, let me encourage you to read this book with the idea of becoming a "winner." The scorecard that you turn into the pro shop will not tell the whole story. Winning will be reflected more in the way you treat your playing partners, or in the outlook you have about life. It is a discipline. It is an attitude. No one is a "born winner." Winning is a mindset that we acquire along the journey—and that may include the lessons we learn in a good round of golf.

Tee it up, hit it straight, and finish the round a *winner*!

~Loren Roberts

INTRODUCTION

Aesop's fable "The Tortoise and the Hare" teaches us from an early age that winners are to be celebrated. Pace and style points may garner praise of lesser significance, but they are nothing compared to being the first to cross the finish line. When the race is over, it always feels good to take a bow in the winner's circle.

As children, we developed a taste for what it means to win. Whether it was from playing *Monopoly* with the family or competing in a baseball game at the neighborhood sandlot, we wanted to come out on top. As parents and teachers have long insisted, "It makes no difference whether you win or lose, but how you play the game." We understood the point, but given the opportunity, we still wanted to win. Nothing could compare to the feeling of being a winner.

Of course, we weren't always victorious in every contest. No one can be the winner all the time. Losing was often the cause for a meltdown, a temper tantrum, or a few choice words mumbled under our breath. It was then we had to learn the lesson of being a good sport and not a sore loser, a lesson that could have been avoided had we only won the game instead of having an "L" plastered on our forehead. Winning was so much more fun.

From my own observations, I am convinced that winners are made, not born. Always moving upward on the learning curve, winners acquire valuable skillsets that enable them to become among the best in their respective fields. They approach life with a positive attitude, focused on accomplishing whatever the immediate task at hand. Winning becomes a matter of personal self-discipline that is perfected over the course of a lifetime.

Some children are gifted with special talents at an early age. Tiger Woods comes to mind. But even Tiger was taught by Earl Woods, his father, who became his son's mentor and biggest fan. Tiger's development as a world champion golfer included his learning new physical skills and life lessons that transformed a young boy into a force to be dealt with in any golf tournament. His collection of trophies attests to his mastery of the game and his mental prowess as a winner.

A common misconception is that for every winner there must be a loser. But that isn't necessarily so. Competition doesn't have to be between individuals or teams vying against one another. It can be, and often is, the contest we have within ourselves. Whenever we compete and can see our own personal growth, whether physical, mental, or spiritual, we become winners. Learning to think in those terms can bring greater satisfaction in life.

10 Essential Thoughts for Winners is a collection of stories, drawn from the golfing world, to illustrate the thought processes that can help us to become winners. From the dreams of Johnny Morris to the uncommon nobility of Byron Nelson, these life lessons have the power to mold us into something more than what we have ever been. Read yourself into the story. Find the application for your own life. Resolve to finish the book with new purpose to make improvements that will shape you into a *winner*!

~ J. Terry Johnson

1

DARE TO DREAM

I love the Ozarks. Having grown up in Springfield, Missouri, my mind harkens back to the days of swimming at Rockaway Beach, fishing the James River, and playing baseball on cow-pasture fields in small towns all over Southwest Missouri. It was an era before the days of air-conditioning and endless television programming. Kids did not come home until it was too dark to play tag or "kick the can." If you liked being outdoors, it was hard to beat the Ozarks.

A century ago, this sparsely populated wilderness was best known as a home for poverty-ravaged hill-billies and lawless moonshiners. Family feuds were real, not just the name of a television game show. That tarnished reputation may have been well earned in generations past, but it hardly describes what the region has become. Tourists by the busloads have transformed a sleepy, backward region of the country into a bustling center of family entertainment, led by a host of live music theaters and countless opportunities for outdoor recreation.

The heartbeat of this transformation has been Branson, Missouri, the state's entertainment showplace. Located forty miles south of Springfield and about ten miles north of the Arkansas state line, this beehive of entrepreneurialism welcomes all who have a few coins to spend. The neon lights in Branson shine almost as brightly as they do on the Strip in Las Vegas.

Locals recall Branson in its early years when the Presley family singers, the Baldknobbers, and the stirring pageant, "Shepherd of the Hills," were the area's main menu for family fun. But when entertainment legends Roy Clark, Glen Campbell, Andy Williams, and the Oak Ridge Boys brought their highly acclaimed musical talents to Branson in the 1980s and 1990s, the boom was on. No longer would "backward" or "simple-minded" define the neighborhood.

Branson had become the trendy destination for millions of tourists from throughout the world.

What followed the music shows to Branson were attractions like Silver Dollar City, a one-of-a-kind amusement park, featuring imaginative rides and spoofs depicting regional history and culture. Soon thereafter, new museums, water parks, and arcades, appealing to families and retirees, were constructed with warp speed. Motels, residential resort communities, and restaurants sprang up around every curve on the twisting roads and highways, built to accommodate enormous increases in vehicular traffic. The region was experiencing growth like it had never seen before.

Enter Johnny Morris. A local boy who grew up in Springfield in the 1950s and 1960s, Morris is a dreamer. He is also an outdoorsman and a conservationist. You may not recognize his name, but you have heard of Bass Pro Shops. That is Johnny Morris's personal enterprise—a boyhood dream he turned into a multi-billion-dollar chain of superstores for people who appreciate nature and its many forms of wildlife.

From his youth, Morris was an avid sportsman. His parents taught him to hunt and fish, but they also taught him about his responsibility to protect the environment, assuring future generations would have the opportunity to enjoy the same experiences he relished as a child. Those early lessons served him well and became the principles by which he chose to operate his successful business empire.

The original Bass Pro outlet was built in 1972, a few blocks from my childhood home in Springfield. It was unlike any other retail store in the marketplace. In search of sporting gear of every imaginable shape, size, and color, a shopper could spend a day walking the aisles and perusing the merchandise without covering half of the showroom's floor space. A major renovation and expansion were completed a few years ago on the "granddaddy store" that now attracts more than four million visitors annually.

Adjacent to the mammoth retail center, Morris has built a Wonders of Wildlife National Museum and Aquarium, two unique galleries that need to be added to every family's "bucket list." Martha and I have toured both, and we can attest that there is nothing quite like them. The museum and the aquarium are spectacular in scale, scope, exhibition, and artistry. The exposition, taken as a whole, has a larger footprint than the Smithsonian Museum of Natural History in Washington, DC.

What does all of this have to do with golf, you might ask? Fair question. Here is the connection. Johnny

Morris has also been dreaming about Branson. He owns thousands of acres of land in the Ozarks and has been developing raw land with big expectations for the region's future.

Thirty years ago, Morris built Big Cedar Lodge, an award-winning resort located on Table Rock Lake, a few miles south of Branson. The property, sprawling over 460 acres, hosts a million visitors each year. It features four restaurants, a luxurious spa, five swimming pools, and packages that include green fees on one or more of the five golf courses affiliated with Big Cedar. Yes! There it is. Golf! The game that is every duffer's delight is thriving in the Ozarks.

By the way, these are not just run-of-the-mill golf courses. May I remind you that Johnny Morris is a dreamer? And that he makes dreams come true! The man who sold fishing tackle from a small display in his father's liquor store and turned it into a $6.5 billion business is on a mission to turn Branson into the world's next "golfing Mecca." Here is how he plans to do it.

Imagine for a moment that you could retain a world-renowned golf architect to design a golf course in your own backyard. Now imagine that you could retain four golfing superstars to do the same. Five courses designed by a PGA Hall of Fame course architect and four of the greatest golfers that have ever played the game.

You have doubts? How about Tom Fazio, Jack Nicklaus, Tiger Woods, Ben Crenshaw, and Gary Player? Those are the men who have designed and built courses in the greater Branson area at the behest of Johnny Morris.

In the fall of 2018, Martha and I spent a few days with her brother and sister-in-law on one of those golf packages at Big Cedar. We stayed four nights at the lodge and were scheduled to play golf at Buffalo Ridge (Fazio), Mountain Top (Player), and Top of the Rock (Nicklaus). Payne's Valley, a new course designed by Tiger Woods and named for the late Payne Stewart, another Springfield native, was still under construction when we visited.

A cold snap had produced a nip in the air and the local agronomist had decided to close Top of the Rock and begin some early winter maintenance. To compensate for our not being allowed to play the jewel that sits atop Big Cedar's rustic property, management allowed us to substitute Ozark National, a new Ben Crenshaw course, which was officially opened to the public two weeks after our trip. The four of us, as it turned out, had the course to ourselves (except for a dozen workers who were putting finishing touches on the bunkers and fairways).

In much the same way as the Wonders of Wildlife Natural Museum and Aquarium is the gold standard of exposition galleries, the golf courses recently built by Morris are first rate in every respect. They have been designed to capture the beauty of the Ozarks and its rugged terrain, with fairways cutting through the foothills, snaking along running creeks, finding their way around limestone outcroppings and native hardwood trees. Sometimes it was hard for us to stay focused on our golf game because we had to stop and pose for another scenic selfie.

The gift of dreaming what others cannot see and turning those dreams into something worthwhile is a cherished asset that belongs to winners. Some of us lack vision; others lack the determination to see their dreams through to reality. Those who possess both vision and the persistence to follow through are the people who get things done. They become winners!

Spend some time with your personal dreams. What would you like to accomplish with the remaining years of your life? Reduce the conceptual ideas to writing. Now, brush the dust off your "bucket list" and identify the next three targets for immediate action.

Winners find a way to advance their unfulfilled goals, even if it means taking baby steps along the way.

Every time I hear the Johnny Morris story, I am encouraged to use my imagination and reach higher for the stars. Retirement can be much more rewarding than spending endless days in a rocking chair. Whether in life or on the golf course, winners inspire me to expand my horizons.

———

"Dream no small dreams for they have no power to move the hearts of men." – **Johann Wolfgang Von Goethe**

2

BECOME SOCIALLY AWARE

Hawaii is host to some of the most amazing golf courses in the world. The island setting is ideal for master course designers to dream indescribable fantasies and make them come true. Even the municipal courses are built in a wonderland of cliffs and waterfalls, lush trees and foliage, and expansive ocean and sky.

My first visit to Hawaii was not for the purpose of playing golf. The men's basketball team at Oklahoma Christian University had been invited to participate in a Christmas holiday tournament hosted by Hawaii Pacific University in Honolulu. Martha and I decided this would be a good opportunity for us to experience a few days in paradise, so we signed up for the tour package with dozens of other basketball fans. It was December 1980.

The basketball games were something less than memorable. The fans from Oklahoma were a small bunch but loud enough to let their presence be known. I honestly do not recall whether we won or lost, but we must not have been crowned champions of the tournament, or I would have remembered the celebration. There was none.

Of course, basketball was simply the excuse for our traveling to Hawaii. It was not the ultimate reason for making the journey. We flew across the Pacific to see Waikiki Beach, Pearl Harbor, Diamondhead, and to watch the native hula dancers shake things up at a beach party luau. We were not disappointed with sites, the roasted pork, or the hula dancers. Oahu was everything we had hoped it would be.

The one "audible" we called on our busy itinerary was a day trip to Maui. A few members of our tour party had made plans to take a morning flight from Honolulu to Kahului and return at dusk. Although we had not heard much about Maui, it sounded like an adventure, so we signed up for the trek and set an early alarm.

Known as the "Valley Isle," Maui is divided into two major sections. Travel guides describe it as a butterfly with two broad wings on either side, separated by a narrow strip of land that includes Kahului, the island's main port city. Haleakala, a dormant volcano ascending 10,000 feet above sea level, is located to the east and is offset by its lesser counterpart, the West Maui Mountains. Since making that initial visit, Maui has become our favorite destination in the Aloha State—a "happy place" away from home.

On a second trip to Maui, Martha and I traveled alone, spending one week in Kihei. A trustee at the university offered us the use of his condo, and we accepted the offer. Again, no golf was scheduled, but we explored the island in greater depth than we had been able to do on the earlier trip. We drove the winding road to Hana, walked its fabled black sand beaches, and swam in the crystal-clear pools at the foot of Haleakala.

It was on that trip Martha and I survived a deadly Pacific tsunami that barreled down on the Hawaiian Islands from the coast of Alaska. Local Hawaiian television stations aired reports that the tidal wave could potentially flood the island beaches, wreaking havoc wherever it happened to strike. The public was warned to seek high ground.

Throughout the morning, helicopters buzzed Maui coastal communities, sounding the alarm for all persons to move to safety. Policemen, driving the seaside roads in patrol cars, used bullhorns to warn of the impending storm. Fishing boats were put out to deeper waters where they could ride atop the huge wave rather than being lashed into the piers by its mighty surge.

Our friend's condo was directly across the highway that ran along the coast near Kihei. A massive tidal wave like the one that struck Hilo on the "Big Island" in 1960 would surely reach our second-floor unit, but for whatever reason, we decided to sit on our balcony and watch this incredible freak of nature. We had seen tornadoes in Oklahoma but had never witnessed a tsunami.

Weather forecasters, using seismic data, were predicting the wave would strike the Maui beaches at approximately 12:00 noon. As the hour drew near, we moved to the outdoor balcony overlooking the ocean and took a seat in the patio chairs. There we sat, patiently watching and waiting.

Martha and I never saw the tsunami. According to the news stations, the wave hit Kahului right on schedule and was officially measured at six inches. We were disappointed in the uneventful storm occurrence. If I could have found one, I would have bought a tee shirt bearing the message, "*We survived the Maui tsunami of 1986.*"

The next time Martha and I returned to Maui we were both into golf. Subsequent trips have always included packing golf clubs, golf clothes, and making tee times at the local courses. On a recent trip, we played five rounds of golf, over five consecutive days, on five different courses. Maui is a golfer's haven.

By far our favorite golfing venue is the Plantation Course at Kapalua. It is no mystery why the PGA has chosen this incredible site as its January opening event, where only the winners from the previous year's PGA tournaments are invited to compete. Plantation has gained a reputation for being the best golf course in Hawaii, and understandably so.

Designed by Bill Coore and Ben Crenshaw and opened to the public in 1991, this amazing golf course sprawls over the foothills of the West Maui Mountains. The slope of its fairways is considerably greater than conventional courses. Spectacular views abound on virtually every hole. Looking west toward Molokai during late winter and early spring, golfers can even observe humpback whales in migration, breaching in the Pailolo Channel that separates the two islands.

One day when Martha and I were scheduled to play Plantation, we found ourselves paired with a single gentleman who happened to be from San Antonio, Texas, only eighty miles south of our home in the Texas Hill Country. He was a retired military colonel who was living out his dream to play this iconic course. We found him to be a good golfer and pleasant company.

What I did not find that day was my golf game. It was not so much that the course was difficult. I knew it would be. That was a given. It was more the fact that golf shots that needed to be accurate both in direction and distance were neither. Bogeys became double bogeys and sometimes triples. One bad hole led to another. Disappointed beyond words, I tallied an uncomfortably high score on the front nine, vowing to do better on the back.

Making the turn at the clubhouse, our threesome trudged up the hill to attack the tenth hole. After losing my drive into the right rough, skulling a fairway wood that landed in a sand bunker, and chunking a wedge that fell pathetically short of the green, my frustration was irrepressible. I slammed the naughty iron back into my bag and muttered a few words under my breath, yet not quietly enough to keep our playing partner from hearing me whine.

What happened next turned out to be one of those "life lessons" that make the game of golf so worthwhile. The astute colonel had heard enough. He said, "Do you mind? Let's stand here for a minute and look out across the ocean."

Martha and I did as he suggested. Molokai was a silhouette on the horizon. Sunbeams bounced off the open water like diamonds sparkling under light. It was a stunning sight.

And then he said more directly to me, "Do you see what I see?" I nodded my head. He added, "Don't allow a bad round of golf to keep you from appreciating one of God's most spectacular gifts of creation."

I was speechless. We stood there—the three of us—just admiring a view that rivals the best nature has to offer. A full-page color photograph in a magazine could not possibly have captured the majesty of what lay before us.

Whining about a golf game has never improved anyone's final score. Everyday life, whether at work or play, is much too short to spend the days complaining about uncomfortable circumstances. Winners have a totally different perspective in those situations. They find the proverbial "silver lining." Furthermore, as I was painfully reminded, grumbling is a rude imposition upon colleagues who must endure the insufferable self-loathing.

As I reflect upon that occasion, the colonel taught me a critical lesson in social awareness. In essence he challenged me to become more observant of my surroundings, to take some time for an attitudinal adjustment. His tutorial was worth every dollar Martha and I had spent for that day's green fees.

Making my way through the back nine, my score didn't get much better, but my appreciation for what really counted in life improved considerably. At the end of the round, we learned that the colonel had recently been diagnosed with terminal cancer. He was playing golf in Hawaii for his last time, and I understood why he was not willing to allow a discontent, fellow Texan ruin the moment.

I never knew what score the colonel tallied on his card that day. He played well—probably bogey golf or better. That was not the point. What mattered was that when he finished the round, he left the course a winner.

We parted the eighteenth green with farewells and good wishes. He has surely moved on by now, but his thoughtful advice remains etched on my heart forever. Winners are not defeated by the untoward circumstances that occur in their lives. They find a way to look at the broader picture.

———

"Earth's crammed with heaven... But only he who sees, takes off his shoes" – **Elizabeth Barrett Browning**

3

SET PROPER PRIORITIES

A few years after retiring to Horseshoe Bay, I wrote a book, *Fairways and Green Pastures*, featuring an imaginary round of golf on Ram Rock, the resort's most intimidating course. Byron Nelson, the PGA Hall of Fame legend, penned the book's foreword. He had played the course on multiple occasions and had fond memories of his visits to the Texas Hill Country.

In *Fairways*, each of the eighteen holes became the backdrop for one of the book's chapters. After describing a particular hole, I segued into a spiritual thought that could be loosely associated with one or more of its unique features. A friend who had heard about the book told me that he had played Ram

Rock many times without ever having had a "spiritual thought"! He had a good point.

The reason I chose Ram Rock as the skeletal structure for the book is because Martha and I happen to own a home on the course. If you ever tee off from the tips on hole number two, you will practically be standing in our back yard. Not too many golfers over the age of thirty choose to hit a drive from our tee box. The hole is a long, difficult par-four, with many opportunities for trouble. Choosing to play from the *professional* tees can be a golfer's worst nightmare.

Some of my friends avoid playing Ram Rock at all. Of the three original Robert Trent Jones, Sr. courses, it is deemed by nearly all golfers to be the most difficult. Water hazards are found on ten holes. All eighteen of the relatively small greens have sand bunkers protecting them and ten holes have sand bunkers in the fairways. Out-of-bounds markers can be seen throughout the course. High scores are a common occurrence.

Yet, there is a distinctive charm associated with Ram Rock. Slicing through the Texas Hill Country, green fairways provide a tailored contrast to the native trees, granite outcroppings, streams, and multi-colored wildflowers. Nothing is more alluring than playing at Horseshoe Bay in the spring when the bluebonnets are in bloom. It is a feast for any golfer's eyes, if not a total distraction.

Adding to the enjoyment of playing Ram Rock is the abundance of wildlife, visible on or near the course. White-tailed deer can be seen loping across the fairways. The blue heron and white egret engage in fishing derbies near the water hazards, while the squirrels and birds chatter to one another in the branches of the native oak trees. On a good day, a golfer might encounter a fox, an armadillo, a road-runner, or a raccoon. The hills are alive with creatures of every shape and size.

Martha and I enjoy playing Ram Rock late in the afternoon when the parade of golfers has begun to wane. You can be sure that neither of us tries to hit our drivers from the tips. We blast away from the shorter tee boxes, hoping we can make the green in three strokes or less. Bogey golf. That is our goal. On the green in three and take a minimum of two putts to finish the hole.

The front nine of Ram Rock concludes with two par-five holes sandwiched around a par-three. Coupled with holes ten and eleven, they become five of the most challenging on the course. When playing these par testers, Martha and I are happy to take any score that is double bogey or down.

One afternoon we had both escaped major damage on the scorecard until we came to the ninth hole: a long par-five that doglegs to the left. Length is the least of the troubles a golfer encounters on number nine. Trees line both sides of the fairway until reaching the 100-yard marker. Then the fairway narrows, and water hazards are on either side. To have any chance at par, an accurate approach shot must be made to a narrow green.

As I drove our golf cart to Martha's ball that day, she began to assess her situation. She had hit a good drive and had followed that with a solid fairway wood, leaving her 140 yards from the center of the green. From her vantage point, the fairway appeared no larger than a ribbon. *Should she lay up with a short iron or take a chance at making the green in regulation?* She decided to go for it.

Using a three-wood, Martha straddled the ball, checked her alignment, and brought her club back and through the ball with good tempo and clubhead speed. *Smack!* The ball lifted above the fairway surface and began its flight toward the green. It appeared to be a good shot, until it became obvious that it wasn't.

Unfortunately, Martha's clubface had been slightly open during her swing causing the ball to cut toward the water hazard on the right. A small fade had become an uncontrollable slice. We both dropped our heads, knowing too well the consequences of an errant shot to the green on hole number nine. *Kerplunk*!

My own third shot had met with more favorable results as I found myself on the green, ready to attempt a twenty-foot birdie putt. I felt chipper about the situation, so I said to Martha, "I have my retriever. Play another ball and I will get the one that you hit into the water." Chivalry was not dead!

After locating the place where the lost ball had likely gone into the hazard, I strained to see if I could locate it beneath the murky water's surface. It appeared there might be two or three balls I could recover, but I needed to position myself a little closer to the edge of the bank. A limb on a nearby tree hung over the water's edge. It was just what I needed to stabilize myself as I reached into the creek with my trusty ball retriever.

Crack!

It was an unwelcomed sound. I knew what was happening, but my body was positioned too far over the water and gravity had begun to take its course. The limb and I hit the water at the same time. Believe me! It was a much louder noise than *kerplunk*.

You would never believe that in this muddy, shallow creek there would be a place where the water was over your head, but I had found one. As much as I wanted to stand up and crawl out of this putrid, smelly drainage ditch, I could not touch bottom, and I did not have enough upper body strength to pull myself up onto the bank. The only option was to dogpaddle twenty feet upstream to an area where the bank was easier to negotiate.

And then the thought struck me! *The only hole on Ram Rock where I have ever seen water snakes is this hole: number nine.*

I hate snakes. Do not try to tell me most of them are harmless. I prefer to keep my distance from all squirming reptiles. *What if I encounter a moccasin before I can extract myself from this dreadful predicament?* The vibes were not good.

About that time, I heard Martha say, "Smile!" Instead of trying to be of any help, she had gone back to the golf cart to retrieve a camera and was laughing as if she were watching a clown perform at the circus. All of this humiliation just to retrieve one of her slightly used golf balls.

No one will ever know if I could have made that birdie putt. Once I managed to crawl up the muddy, sloped bank that led back to the fairway, I dried the water from my face with a towel, hopped into our cart, and headed home. I was miserable. And the stench from that putrid water! Spare me the memory.

Since the day of my unpleasant experience on Ram Rock's hole number nine, I have reassessed some of my priorities. Safety is important. A lost golf ball is not. Moccasins belong in the water. I do not. Chivalry is honorable. Making a fool of myself is not.

And thus, we learn there are priorities pertaining to most aspects of our lives. Some things are important, and some things are trivial. Winners know the difference between the two and make judgments accordingly.

I am much less concerned today about a lost golf ball than I used to be. Losing one is not a life and death proposition. Facing a water moccasin in a smelly pool of water, on the other hand, might be a perilous occurrence. It is all about managing choices and applying common sense.

By the way, Martha has renamed Ram Rock's hole number nine. She says it shall forever be known as "The Johnson Baptismal Gardens."

———

"To change your life, you need to change your priorities" – **Mark Twain**

4

BE HONEST TO A FAULT

Baseball rules are enforced by umpires, and football infractions are yellow flagged by referees. They are the impartial arbiters of the game. Once an official makes the call, appropriate adjustments are made, and the game moves on to the next play.

Golf, on the other hand, requires players to impose penalties on themselves whenever they breach the game's sacred code of conduct. Playing golf by the rules demands an extra measure of personal integrity, not expected of the participants in other sports. Can you imagine Michael Jordan ever feeling obliged to hand the ball over to the opposing team after stepping on the out-of-bounds line, when no one on the playing court saw him do it? Neither can I.

The venerable Bobby Jones, golf's most celebrated amateur and a legend of the game, was a lawyer by profession. His law practice provided the income necessary for him to pursue his passion: playing golf. A child phenom with any golf club in his hand, Jones won his first tournament at age six on his home course, the East Lake Golf Club in Atlanta, Georgia. He won his first major amateur championship when he was fourteen and chose to retire from competitive golf at twenty-eight, an age when most golfers are in their prime.

During his brief golfing career, Jones won four U.S. Open Championships and three Open Championships (British Open), competing against the best professionals of his day. He also won a host of amateur tournaments and led the American team to five victories in the biennial Walker Cup competition between amateurs from the United States and their counterparts from Great Britain and Ireland. He was always an intense competitor, playing ferociously to win.

But the story that reveals the heart of Bobby Jones is told about his honesty as a participant in the 1925 U.S. Open. While addressing his ball on an approach shot early in the tournament, Jones's club brushed the grass, unintentionally causing the ball to move. No one saw the tiny movement except for him. Nonetheless, he called a one-stroke penalty on himself and advised his playing partner and the U.S.G.A. officials of the infraction. That one extra shot cost him the tournament. He eventually lost to Willie Macfarlane in a playoff that never would have been necessary if it were not for the penalty stroke added to his scorecard in the first round. When praised for his honesty, his classic response was, "You might as well praise me for not robbing banks."

The Rules of Golf is a handbook filled with rules, regulations, and technicalities that govern the way the game is designed to be played. A typical weekend golfer who competes for the social benefit and his own personal pleasure may choose to interpret the rules loosely, abiding by the spirit while ignoring the minutia. A professional golfer, on the other hand, is obliged to play strictly by the book. Rules establish the parameters of fairness on the course, assuring equal treatment for all competitors.

A few years ago, Martha and I attended a dinner hosted by the Fellowship of Christian Athletes in Austin, Texas. We were guests of our friends, Reagan and Debbie Lambert, who headed the organization's

Austin chapter for more than thirty years. At the banquet, students and coaches from the local high schools testified to the "value added" benefits brought to athletic competition by FCA. It was both an informative and an enjoyable evening.

Reagan had invited Webb Simpson, a popular PGA champion, to be the keynote speaker for the event. Martha and I knew Simpson's name, but little more than that. We came away considerably more knowledgeable about him as a person, as a golfer, and as a man of faith. He was impressive. Since then, he has become one of our favorites to follow on the PGA Tour.

Simpson, a native of North Carolina, has had his share of success playing professional golf. The Wake Forest graduate won the U.S. Open in 2012, the prestigious Players Championship in 2018, and a shelf full of other trophies to adorn his den. He has also represented the United States in both the Ryder Cup and the President's Cup international team events. At every level of play, Simpson has proven himself a winner.

As important as winning is to any serious athlete, Simpson does not live by a code of "win at any cost." In 2011, he, much like Bobby Jones, found himself in one of those situations where he had to call a one-stroke penalty on himself—one that eventually cost him a tournament victory. Here is the gist of what he told the audience at the FCA dinner.

Going into the final round of the Zurich Classic at the TPC Louisiana Course in Avondale, Louisiana, Simpson shared the lead with Bubba Watson. Watson, a perennial fan favorite, struggled on the front nine, while Simpson lit up the course. Simpson, hungry to win his first PGA Tour title, pulled three strokes ahead of Watson at the eleventh hole and was leading him by one stroke going into the fifteenth. Victory was in sight.

As Simpson stood over a one-foot putt for par on the fifteenth green, a gust of wind caused the ball to move ever so slightly. Simpson had already grounded his putter on the green's surface before the movement occurred. The rule was clear. If the ball moves after the club has been grounded, even if the club did not cause the ball's movement, the player must be assessed a one-stroke penalty. There was nothing Simpson could do but call the infraction, make his short putt for a bogey, rather than a par, and move on to the next hole.

The round concluded with Simpson and Watson tied. The two men engaged in a playoff that Watson won on the second hole. Watson's first-place prize money was $1,152,000; Simpson's second-place check was for $460,800. Had the self-imposed penalty not come into play, he would have been the outright champion at the end of regulation play. Competing strictly by the rules cost him almost $700,000. The next year, the U.S.G.A. changed the rule about ball movement caused by wind—no penalty is assessed if the player was not responsible in any way for the ball's movement.

Most casual golfers have a general understanding of the rules but have not taken the time to study them in depth. In social play, the rules are what the group says they are. Some allow a mulligan on the first drive of the round. A putt may be considered a "gimme" if it is "within the leather" (i.e., fewer inches away from the cup than the length of the padded grip of a club). Maximum score on any hole may be set at net double bogey. Even courses are known to have local rules that make exceptions to the official "Rules of Golf."

Unfortunately, even when a loose interpretation of the rules is in play, there are still those who compete within the construct of the game, and those who choose to do otherwise. In other words, they cheat! They shave their score by a stroke or two, recording a five on the scorecard, although, in fact, they took six strokes to finish the hole. When no one is looking, they may improve their lie on a shot from the rough or ground their club in a hazard, both requiring penalties to be assessed in most golfing circles.

Golfers who cheat soon develop a reputation for being dishonest. Other players know who the cheaters are, even among the professionals. And once a person has a name for being untruthful in competition, at any level of play, it becomes difficult to change the tarnished image. Word of dishonorable behavior has a way of circulating. Cheaters are never considered to be good company on the golf course.

Every generation has paid tribute to the value of being honest. One of the more frequently quoted sayings is attributed to Aesop: "Honesty is the best policy." Indeed, it is.

Where truth and honest behavior are in play, the arena is both immaterial and at the same time universal. Whether on the golf course or in the boardroom, being truthful matters. Being a person who tells the truth speaks more to who we are than the many achievements and awards listed in our résumé.

Honesty is inherent in the DNA of winners.

━━

"Honesty is the first chapter in the book of wisdom" –Thomas Jefferson

5

MODEL MODESTY

Everyone enjoys a nice surprise, whether it is the arrival of an unexpected gift or a friend who drops by for a visit. It puts a smile on one's face. It lifts the spirit. It provides a pleasurable moment to recall.

Some surprises are contrived, planned well in advance. A good writer develops a storyline with multiple sub-plots and then delights the reader by bringing them all together in an unpredictable finale. Surprise!

A wife plans a dinner party for her husband's birthday but keeps it a secret until he arrives at the restaurant and sees his friends. Surprise!

Or a young man hides an engagement ring in the ribbons of a corsage. Surprise!

Other unanticipated events, however, are more spontaneous. They just occur! Who could possibly have seen them coming?

On a beautiful morning in June, Martha and I were enjoying a perfect day for golf in Maui. The sun was shining. The trade winds were light. Trailing white clouds provided a stunning contrast against the azure blue sky. We could not have asked for better weather to play our first round of golf on Kapalua's magnificent Bay Course.

Although Plantation is more universally known than Bay, its sister course, there is nothing shabby about taking second place in this contest. Other than its length and spectacular vistas from a higher elevation, Plantation has nothing on its coastal neighbor to the west. Both are endowed with lush vegetation and eye-popping views. Plantation commands the West Maui Mountain foothills while Bay hugs the Pacific Ocean along Maui's northwest coast.

On this particular morning, the queue at the starter's box was considerably longer than I had hoped it would be. Martha and I took a few swings on the driving range, working on tempo and making good contact with the ball. Then we moved to the practice green to test our hand with the putter. The greens appeared to be faster than the ones we were used to playing at home, but our objective on most putts was merely to get them "cozy-cozy," near the hole.

Now seated in the golf cart, we waited patiently for our number to be called. After sending a foursome off the first tee, the starter began walking toward our cart. He greeted us with a smile, introduced himself, and confirmed our tee time. We exchanged pleasantries, learning that the man had retired from a job in Pennsylvania five years ago. Then he asked, "Do you mind if I add a single to your round?" We assured him that was acceptable. He thanked us and walked away.

Shortly before our scheduled tee time, the starter approached us again, this time with a middle-aged female at his side. She was an attractive woman, dressed in fashionable golf attire, complete with Walter Genuin shoes. Martha noticed the shoes. I had no clue.

The starter said, "This is Ms. Evans. She will be joining you this morning." The woman extended her hand and said, "Hello. I'm Kathryn Evans." We greeted her with smiles, explained that we were visiting from Texas and playing the Bay course for the first time.

Kathryn told us that her son lived in Maui and that she had played Bay many times. She also mentioned a trip she had made to the Austin area exploring the sites depicted in S. C. Gwynne's novel, *Empire of the Summer Moon.* That piqued our interest because we too had read *Empire*, a riveting story about the struggles between Comanche Indians and German settlers in central Texas during the 1800s. The introductions had gone well. Now it was time to play golf.

As expected, Kathryn was a much more accomplished golfer than Martha and I were. Her swing was smooth, and her shots consistently landed in the fairway. We both admired her poise around the greens. She carried herself as someone who was comfortably confident in her golf game.

Over the course of the round, conversation began to flow more freely, and we gently probed into one another's respective lives. Martha and I shared that we had met while attending college, and that we had two married daughters and seven grandchildren. She volunteered that her mother's name was Martha and that she had a sister who was also named Martha. We inquired if they were golfers. She said they were not, but both were into cooking.

Kathryn also mentioned that she played golf in Palm Springs with a woman from the Texas Hill

Country. The woman's name was Luann Sewell. Martha squealed, "We know Luann and Bob Sewell. I play golf with her at Horseshoe Bay." Small world. We made a mental note to share the experience with Luann upon our return home.

Martha and I came to the eighteenth green totally exhausted. The course was magnificent, but we had searched all day for our "A-game." It was nowhere to be found.

Kathryn had been delightful as a playing partner. We thanked each other for mutual cordiality, bid our adieus, and drove our golf carts to the bag drop at the parking lot. There, Martha and I loaded our clubs into the car and drove back to the Westin Kaanapali Ocean Resort Villas.

Upon returning to Texas, Martha ordered two pairs of Walter Genuin shoes and had her eyes on another pair featured on the website. They were a step up from her closet full of Footjoys. She also called Luann Sewell to tell her about meeting Kathryn in Maui. Now here came the surprise.

Luann acknowledged her friendship with Kathryn and then said, "You know who she is, don't you?" Martha was taken aback, but hesitantly said, "No. Should I?" Luann replied, "Kathryn is Martha Stewart's sister."

Only then did the pieces begin to fall into place. Dressed to the nines. A sister named Martha, who liked to cook. Of course, this made perfect sense. But why didn't Kathryn tell us her sister was the fashionable icon, Martha Stewart?

There may have been multiple reasons for Kathryn's keeping her sister's identity a secret when among strangers on the golf course. My hunch is that her own modesty dissuaded her from bragging about having a famous sibling. She did not need to use Martha Stewart's celebrity status to make herself appear more important to others. Some bits and pieces of personal information are best left unmentioned.

Modesty is a virtue that needs to be revived in today's culture. At a time when competitive instincts drive individuals to promote themselves incessantly through social media, it is refreshing whenever humility is on display. To gloat over personal achievements, advancements, or acquisitions is a sign of insecurity. Winners know that. They have learned the art of talking less about themselves while shining the light on others.

It is unlikely my life's journey will ever intersect Kathryn Evans's path again. She is simply one of those strangers Martha and I encountered on a golf course years ago. A person to remember. A lesson to treasure.

———

"He who speaks without modesty will find it difficult to make his words good" – **Confucius**

6

KEEP A CLEAR CONSCIENCE

Golf courses do not just happen. They are the work product of inventive minds that take raw tracts of land and envision what an acreage might become by adding winding fairways, smooth putting greens, contoured sand bunkers, and testy water hazards. These dreamers see what mere mortals could never imagine. And then one day, like sprinkling fairy dust on an unimproved acreage, a sprawling golf course emerges.

The original three golf courses at Horseshoe Bay Resort were designed by the world-renowned course architect Robert Trent Jones, Sr. Slick Rock opened to the public in 1973, and Ram Rock and Apple

Rock came on board in 1981 and 1985, respectively. All are stellar courses, continuing to rank annually as three of the best in Texas.

In late 2012, Summit Rock, a new golf course designed by Jack Nicklaus, one of golf's most celebrated champions, opened at Horseshoe Bay. The course's name is derived from its elevated terrain overlooking the relatively small Texas Hill Country community and its more substantial neighboring amenity, Lake LBJ. The panoramic views are stunning, with vistas extending twenty miles to the north and west. Summit has become the course of choice for Martha and me. A course we have come to call "home."

Nicklaus was present on a warm, sunny day in October for the 2012 grand opening of Summit Rock. At a luncheon under a huge tent, Martha and I joined with other founding members to hear the man of the moment speak and answer questions from the audience. We were captivated by his account of the design process and the collective effort required to turn raw concepts into something spectacular.

To our delight, Nicklaus agreed to play a few holes on the new course as a teaching demonstration for the luncheon guests. He teed the ball up on four holes, beginning on two of Summit's more difficult:

numbers ten and eleven. Prior to each shot, Nicklaus described his thought process for attacking the hole, providing keen insight into a professional golfer's innermost thoughts.

Hardly breaking a sweat, Nicklaus birdied holes ten and eleven, and then parred number twelve, a challenging par-three. The small crowd of spectators was abuzz with admiration for the veteran's mastery of the new course. He made the game appear to be so simple.

Nicklaus approached the thirteenth hole with a bit of caution. Some golfers can reach this relatively short, par-four hole with a long drive. No one doubted the "Golden Bear" could do so if he tried, but on this day, he chose to play the hole more conventionally.

Using an iron, Nicklaus hit his drive into the middle of the fairway, leaving himself about one hundred yards short of the green. His second shot, a lofted sand-wedge, settled safely on the putting surface, but roughly twenty feet away from the cup. He would need to make that putt for another birdie.

After surveying the contour of the green and aligning the putt, Nicklaus sent the ball on its way, dropping it straight into the cup. The adoring fans went wild. The golf legend had once again lived up to his reputation.

Since that memorable day, Martha and I have played hundreds of rounds on Summit Rock. She plays every Thursday with a competitive women's group; I play Wednesdays with some of my high-handicap buddies. While the camaraderie is good, my game always leaves room for improvement. Yet, I never tire of playing the course.

The weekly contest with the men's group is a blast. A good day for any of us is a round in the nineties. If we happen to break into the eighties, the celebration can be heard all the way to Lake LBJ.

The founder and "commissioner" of our weekly band of duffers is Cully Exsted, a Minnesotan who found his way to warmer climate for his retirement years. We all like Cully. He is good company and an able competitor. Each week he polls the group via email to determine who will play. Then he selects the teams, sets up the scoring rules for the day, and collects a modest ante from each player.

One afternoon in late February, I was paired with Phil Schoch, one of the better golfers in our group. We share common work experiences and mutual acquaintances from prior years spent in Oklahoma. Four times out of five, Phil shoots a score that's lower than mine, but on this day, we were teammates, not rivals.

Unfortunately, I was not having one of my better outings. The dreaded "shank shot" had found its way into my bag, running up the score and depressing my spirits. Phil had seen enough of my errant shots and had listened to my endless whining. He knew that unless I could make a turnaround on the back nine, our team was not going to be in the money.

The par-four eleventh is one of the more spectacular holes on the course. Tee boxes are situated at the top of the summit, commanding a view of Packsaddle Mountain and the lake in the distance. The fairway has a gradual descent for three hundred yards to a shallow ravine, from which it is another one hundred yards to the green. For our group, the hole usually requires a drive and a layup shot short of the gully before trying to approach the pin.

To my delight, I had hit the perfect layup in front of the hazard and had visions of using my faithful nine-iron to land a third shot close to the flag. Phil had an exceptionally long drive that day and had already hit his second shot over the hazard but not quite to the green.

"I'll just walk across and meet you on the other side," Phil said, as he made his way through the ravine's rocks and underbrush.

The hazard normally has a spring-fed stream flowing through its tall grasses and prickly bramble making a stroll across the obstacle virtually impossible. But this year the weather had been unusually dry causing the springs to dry up and the stream to stop flowing. Phil had no trouble getting across to the other side.

Now it was time for me to hit that approach shot. I checked my Garmin watch for the distance, gathered myself over the ball, and swung that nine-iron as if there were no tomorrow. To my utter dismay, the ball dribbled into the hazard and lodged in a tall clump of grass. Steam was coming out my ears. I walked into the hazard, flailed at the ball one more time, and returned to my golf cart disgusted and murmuring ugly thoughts.

What possessed me to do what I did next is shrouded in mystery. After throwing my club into the golf bag, I climbed into the cart, drove it straight through the dry-as-a-bone hazard, and then sped onto the cart path on the other side. Something inside said, that was not a smart thing to do, but at that moment I was too upset with myself to care. A bad day on the course had only gotten worse.

Mercifully, the round ended. Our team did not win. There was no celebration in the clubhouse. At best, we had survived to play another day. I did notice, however, that Cully was having a serious conversation with our club pro who appeared to be somewhat upset. I wondered what that was all about. It did not take long for me to find out.

Cully, using exceptional diplomacy, approached me, and said, "Apparently, someone in our group was reported for driving a golf cart through the hazard on hole number eleven." A pang of conscience rattled me to the core.

"Oh, Cully, I'm sorry," I confessed. "I was the one who did that." He did not look overly surprised.

And then I said, "Shall I say something to Dell?"

"Don't worry about it," Cully reassured me. "He does not know who drove across and I told him I would take care of the matter. I have and it's done."

I thanked Cully for shouldering the load but drove home ashamed of myself for juvenile misbehavior. The last time I could remember feeling this way was when my third-grade teacher sent me to the principal's office.

Living with a guilty conscience is a wretched feeling. It haunts. It stings. It foreshadows future, unpleasant encounters with people who have been affected by the wrongdoing. Unable to stomach the shame for more than an hour, I picked up the telephone and called the Summit Rock pro shop.

"Dell," I began my apology, "I just wanted you to know that I was the schmuck who drove the golf cart through the hazard this afternoon." *Crickets* on the other end.

"Cully said you did not know who it was," I continued, "but I didn't want you to think that it might have been one of the other players in our group. I knew better at the time and promise I will never do it again." Much to my relief, the apology was graciously accepted, and a nagging burden was lifted.

Winners have their faults. Sometimes they make stupid mistakes. But they know the difference between right and wrong, never trying to defend their own bad behavior at the expense of the truth. They deal with their shortcomings and make amends where they can or restitution, if necessary.

An old proverb goes something like this: "A guilty conscience needs no accuser." So true. I rarely play the eleventh hole at Summit Rock without being reminded of that lesson.

———

"Labor to keep alive in your breast that little spark of celestial fire called conscience"– **George Washington**

7

EMPLOY GOOD HUMOR

Gaillardia is the name of Oklahoma's state wild-flower. The daisy-like bloomer featuring varying shades of red and yellow can be found throughout the Sooner State, gracing lawns and gardens. Also known as the "blanket flower," Gaillardia was named years ago in honor of a French botanist, Gaylord de Marentonneau.

Three generations of the Edward Gaylord family have been the linchpins of civic leadership in Oklahoma City. They are direct descendants of the noted French botanist and have been a credit to his name. Among their ownership interests have been the Oklahoma Publishing Company (*The*

Daily Oklahoman); the "Grand Ole Opry"; and the Opryland properties in Nashville, Tennessee, and the Broadmoor Resort in Colorado Springs, Colorado. Other family enterprises have included major radio and television stations across the nation and commercial real estate ventures in several states.

In the 1990s, Edward L. Gaylord, who at the time was head of the family's business conglomerate, decided to develop a parcel of farmland in northwest Oklahoma City into a residential golf course community. He named the project Gaillardia. The course and then its stylish, three-story clubhouse opened in 1998 and 1999, respectively.

Spread over 250 acres of gentle rolling prairie, Gaillardia is a links course that was designed by Arthur Hills. The PGA Senior Tour (now the PGA Tour Champions) has used this venue twice for its year-ending tournament where all event winners during the season compete for the final championship. Tom Gilder (2001) and Tom Watson (2002) prevailed in those early contests.

Gaillardia has also played host to the popular television series, *Shell's Wonderful World of Golf*. On a beautiful Tuesday morning in September 2000, Phil Mickelson and Fred Couples competed in a stroke play Shell match, with the winner taking home $100,000 and the loser $50,000. Jack Whitaker and Judy Rankin were on the microphones. I was fortunate to be in the gallery as a guest of the Gaylord family.

Judy Rankin set the tone for the day on the first tee box where she conducted a brief interview with the two competitors. She teased Mickelson about being the "challenger," noting that Couples had won five straight Shell matches, while Phil had lost all three of his prior attempts (losing to Ernie Els, Colin Montgomerie, and Tom Lehman). She suggested that "Lefty" might have something to prove. Indeed, he did.

Never had I been able to stand so close to a professional golfer while he was plying his skills with a club in his hands. The setting was embarrassingly intimate. These well-known stars of the golfing community jested casually with each other and even drew spectators into their conversations. It felt more like a family reunion than a sports match.

The first hole was a 440-yard, par-four with sand bunkers guarding either side of the fairway. Both men launched prodigious drives, avoiding the bunkers, and rolling out to within one hundred and twenty yards of the green. The small crowd responded with a chorus of *oohs* and *aahs*, and the match was underway.

When Fred Couples swings a golf club, it is art in motion. The tempo is perfect. The movement is effortless. No one would ever know that the man suffers from a cranky back. But on that particular day, Couples's game was slightly off. Masterful shots were not being rewarded with correspondingly good results.

Mickelson, on the other hand, was on a tear. He was bombing his drives 300-yards or more on fairway after fairway. The front nine at Gaillardia had two par-five holes. One played 562 yards and the other 556 yards. Mickelson eagled both.

As the professional rivals approached the par-three ninth hole, Mickelson held a decisive five-stroke lead. A new tee box had been made especially for this event. It lay 245 yards from the green. Mickelson took a two-iron and landed his drive six feet from the pin. This appeared to be the day for his first Shell Challenge victory.

At the turn, Judy Rankin again conducted a brief interview with the contestants. Mickelson was modest about his play, noting that he had held leads in earlier Shell matches, but those leads had not stood up on the back nine. He also praised Couples' reputation for putting together strings of four or five birdies in a row. He was taking nothing for granted.

Couples was in a much lighter mood. The day happened to be his wedding anniversary. He asked Mickelson to have some mercy on a man who was experiencing such an emotional moment in his life. Everyone had a good laugh, and we were off to the tenth tee box.

The back nine was reminiscent of the front. Both men hit impressive drives; Mickelson's always happened to roll out several yards farther than Couples's. On the 597-yard par-five fourteenth hole, Couples hit his drive 347 yards; Mickelson's traveled 397 yards. At that point, Couples yelled to Lefty, "How's the view from down there?" The crowd loved it.

No one carded an eagle on the final nine holes. Pars and birdies filled the scorecard. That was the primary difference between the back and what Mickelson had been able to accomplish on the front.

Both men were walking at a gait that suggested they were in much better physical shape than those of us in the crowd. Many of the spectators were working hard to keep pace. I had thoroughly enjoyed the day, but my "dogs" were barking. It was time to wrap up this friendly contest and head for home.

The eighteenth hole at Gaillardia is a 540-yard par-five that plays downhill. The fairway is split in the middle by a water drainage creek. The left side is more direct to the green, but much narrower than the open area to the right. Both men chose to hit drives left of the water hazard, appearing unconcerned about the tightness of the fairway. Again, they hit magnificent drives, Mickelson's traveling at least thirty yards farther than Couples's.

Before hitting his second shot, Couples engaged a young boy from the crowd in a brief conversation. Joking about how Mickelson had been outdriving him all day, Couples suggested the lad should join the professional golf circuit in a few years and teach "Lefty" a lesson. He went on to tell the boy that he suspected Mickelson would travel home on his private plane, telling everyone how much farther his own drives had gone than those hit by Couples. It was a light moment that provided some insight into the core character of this championship golfer.

The last putts of the round resulted in birdies for both competitors. Mickelson, however, had dominated the match, having finally achieved his first Shell Challenge victory. Checks were awarded, smiles all around. The host was thanked profusely, the audience applauded, and then dispersed. It had been a delightful day at Gaillardia.

Looking back on that experience, I remember the sensational golf played by two professional champions, but I also recall the little things that made both men winners. They were humble and accessible. They were cordial toward one another and surprisingly friendly with the small gathering of spectators. And they both had a sense of humor.

A little humor can go a long way toward eliminating barriers that exist between people from different social strata. Couples and the grade school lad on hole eighteen were just two chums on the course, enjoying a visit. Age and talent were irrelevant. Each was enjoying the moment on a level playing field.

And so, I thought to myself, a nation that is divided on a broad array of generationally divergent issues could take a lesson from what I had witnessed at Gaillardia. A measure of humor and a cup of human kindness can help build goodwill among people who may not have that much in common. Winners have learned to lead others by employing those admirable personality traits. Just another lesson from the golf course.

———

"A sense of humor is part of the art of leadership, of getting along with people, of getting things done"

– Dwight D. Eisenhower

8

Make Memories

Most people of a certain age remember where they were in 1963 when President John F. Kennedy was assassinated. Many can recall "Nine-Eleven," that fateful day in 2001 when morning television programs were interrupted by graphic footage of terrorists flying commercial airplanes into Manhattan skyscrapers. A few will even remember the night in 1969 when they sat glued to the television set, watching astronaut Neil Armstrong walk on the moon. Memory is a valuable bench marker in our lives.

Playing a round of golf with good friends can also become the subject of a lifetime memory. Who does not remember a first round of golf at Pebble Beach?

Or walking the fairways at Augusta National? Or the day they shot a hole-in-one on any par-three hole, regardless of the yardage? Those images are permanently etched into a golfer's mind and are available for instant mental replay, with or without embellishment.

Honestly, I cannot say that I have ever experienced the joy of scoring an ace on a three-par, and I have yet to lay eyes on Augusta National. But I have played Pebble Beach. It is, after all, a public course. Anyone who can afford the hefty greens fee (plus caddy and tip) can reserve a spot on the starter's tee sheet. Over the years, this legendary course has hosted internationally acclaimed athletes, award-winning Hollywood film stars, barons of industry, and heads-of-state from nations all over the world. Thankfully, it has also allowed some of us in lower echelons to realize our own golfing dreams on its fabled fairways.

At a dinner honoring Martha and me for years of administrative service at Oklahoma Christian University, the Board of Trustees rewarded us with a golf package to Pebble Beach. We were stunned by the surprise but quickly accepted the gesture of good will and began making plans to cash in the voucher. I spent a few weeks honing my golf skills on the practice range in anticipation of the trip, while Martha chose to spend her time shopping for a new golfing wardrobe.

Pebble Beach Golf Links, located near Carmel, California, on the Monterey Peninsula, is more than the number one public golf course in America. It has few rivals, whether public or private courses, in the world. From the opening drive off the number one tee box, to the closing shots on hole eighteen, a round of golf on this eye-popping site is an adventure in fantasyland. Mind blowing!

The nation's fascination with golf at Pebble Beach began years ago when in 1947, popular crooner, movie star idol, and golfing enthusiast Bing Crosby agreed to resurrect his fashionable pro-am tournament at Pebble Beach Golf Links and its sister Monterrey courses. Crosby had hosted his first charity pro-am in San Diego in 1937, but the "Clambake," as it had become known, was suspended in 1942 because of World War II. At Pebble Beach, the resuscitated event became so popular that ABC Sports agreed to televise the 1958 Bing Crosby National Pro-Am nationwide, and the rest became a chapter in golf history.

The Crosby Clambake was more than just another golf tournament. It was a party like no other on the PGA circuit. In the years prior to 1977, when

Crosby died playing golf in Spain, he had chosen 200 well-heeled, amateur golfers from more than 8,000 applicants who sought to participate in the annual charity event. That alone spoke volumes about the tournament's uncommon popularity.

Many factors contributed to the Crosby Clambake's appeal. Playing alongside the nation's elite golfers was an attraction. Walking the fairways of Pebble Beach had its allure. So did the festivities that followed each round. But the underlying motive for most of these celebrities, who were contributing thousands of dollars to charity for an opportunity to play Crosby's tournament, was nothing more than to have fun.

Golf has its social component. So does life. Celebration with friends is good tonic for the soul. You can be sure the Clambake participants went home with stories to tell friends and family and plenty of souvenirs commemorating the occasion. Photographs were framed or mounted in albums for all to see. More than anything else, that weekend was about making memories.

Which brings me back to that unforgettable trip to Carmel in 1996, the day Martha and I first experienced the ecstasy of walking the hallowed grounds of Pebble Beach. We were awestruck, feeling unworthy to step foot on the big stage. Yet, there we were, checking into the resort's hotel, trying to hide an overwhelming sense of awe and intimidation.

Martha's older brother, Brooks Mitchell, and his wife Vickie were our traveling companions. I could write a lengthy chapter about our golfing escapades with the two of them. Brooks is affectionately known as "Bubba," and there are many good reasons why friends and family use that moniker. He was the only one of our foursome to have already played Pebble Beach. The rest of us were newbies.

Because we arrived at the resort at dusk, we had been unable to see much of the property before retiring to our rooms. I spent an hour or more reading every pamphlet, instructions sheet, and other papers that had been given to us at the front desk. The small room was comfortable and quiet, but the buzz in my head would not go away. Martha laid out her golfing garb for the morning round, while I set a travel alarm, and we called it a night.

Having gained two hours on the clock by traveling to the West Coast the day before, we found it easy to bounce out of bed at the crack of dawn. The first thing I did was open the window shade to check on the day's weather. All was good: plenty of sunshine and no rain in the forecast. We suited up, ate a light breakfast, and rendezvoused with Brooks and Vickie at the first tee box.

I will spare you a hole-by-hole synopsis of our march around the course. Those details are neither important nor the things I remember when my mind flashes back to Pebble Beach. The course's record low round was never in jeopardy. No eagles nor birdies were entered on our scorecard, but we did come home with a bushelful of memories.

For example, after finishing our putts on hole two, we noticed the club's ground crew had felled an enormous Cypress tree that for years had guarded the left side of the fairway. We pride ourselves in knowing that the four of us hold the "record" for being the last golfers to play Pebble Beach with that Cypress still standing. We have waited to hear Jim Nance or Sir Nick Faldo drop that historical tidbit into their "golf salad" when broadcasting the annual AT&T Pebble Beach Pro-Am. No mention to date.

Prior to playing the third hole, Martha fell on a cart path curb, causing a knot the size of a golf ball to swell up on her right forearm. We thought she might have broken a bone, but since she could still swing a club and was unwilling to say, "quit," we all decided not to allow her misfortune to cast a pall on such a glorious day at Pebble Beach.

The shortest and arguably the most picturesque hole on the course is number seven, a downhill, three-par that juts precipitously into the ocean. Sam Snead, the winningest professional golfer of his time, once used a putter to strike his first shot from the tee box because heavy winds were playing havoc with any ball hit with a lofted club. His ball ran down the cart path and onto the green, where he took two more putts to par the hole. Much to my delight, I also carded a par on the seventh hole. It was my only par recorded for the round, and no, I did not use my putter off the tee box.

Twenty-five years have passed since our storied trip to Pebble Beach. The four of us talk about it as if it occurred six months ago. We share the memory of a common experience: the excitement of walking the same fairways where golfing legends have made PGA history; the terror of hitting golf shots on holes abutting the ocean; the satisfaction of realizing a life-long dream. They are part of our memory bank, a reservoir of blessings for a lifetime.

Bob Hope, Bing Crosby's friend and co-star in the Hollywood "Road" films, is well known for his theme song, "Thanks for the Memory." Both men hosted charity-golf events that produced many price-less memories for their friends. My observation is that winners have a way of making memories, preserving them, and sharing them with others.

———

"Memories of our lives, of our works and our deeds will continue in others" – **Rosa Parks**

9

FINISH STRONG

W hen selecting a state that has great golf courses, Wisconsin may not be the one at the top of the list. Likely, it is not even in the top ten. "Cheese Country" sounds too far north—too close to the Canadian border or to the Artic Circle, for that matter.

And forget about playing golf in the Badger State year-round. Winters are too severe, preventing even the most avid golfers from playing when a twelve-inch snow covers the ground. Can you remember the "Ice Bowl" in Green Bay in 1967? Be assured, the Dallas Cowboys can, and do.

But consider these factors for a moment. The 2017 U.S. Open was held at Erin Hills, one of the top ten public golf courses in the United States; Sand Valley Resort recently opened three, nationally award-winning courses in Nekoosa, Wisconsin (wherever that is); and then there is Whistling Straits, a Pete Dye creation that has been compared favorably with elite golf courses from all over the world.

The Straits and its sister course, the Irish, can be found about ten miles north of Kohler and Sheboygan, Wisconsin. It was fashioned after the coastal courses in Ireland, featuring grassy sand dunes, treacherous fairway pot bunkers, and a roaming herd of Scottish, black-faced sheep. From the tips it measures 7790 yards with a slope rating of 152-77.2. When a golfer plays the Straits, he gets more than his money's worth.

Designed as a links course, not many trees populate this rolling hillside. Nonetheless, the Straits has an appeal of its own. Eight of the holes have a view of Lake Michigan and more than 900 strategically placed sand bunkers dot the rolling landscape. If you play the course, bring your camera.

Martha and I were introduced to Whistling Straits by our daughter and son-in-law who bought a package for us to play three rounds of golf and spend three nights at the American Club Resort Hotel in Kohler. We had no idea what to expect. Had it not been for the 2010 PGA Championship having been played at the Straits, the course may have flown beneath our radar screen.

Ah, yes! The 2010 PGA Championship that is best remembered for the shocking controversy on the 72nd and final hole of regulation play. For those who like suspenseful endings, this tournament ranks among the best.

Dustin Johnson, much younger and less experienced than the superstar he has become, was the center of attention and leading the tournament going into his final hole on Sunday. His wayward drive from the eighteenth tee began a sequence of events that created a stir throughout the golfing world. Golf Channel and ESPN replayed the video continuously.

It all began when Johnson's drive ventured far right of the fairway, landing amid a throng of spectators in a sandy patch of grass and dirt. Fortunately, the ball was neither lost nor out-of-bounds. It was playable, but an approach shot of slightly more than 200 yards was required for Johnson to make the green in regulation. After assessing the situation, he opted for a four-iron and asked his caddie to clear spectators from his line of flight to the green. This was when the buzz began.

What appeared to be a barren patch of dirt and sand was actually one of those 900-plus bunkers that, according to a local, posted rule, was to be played as a hazard. According to PGA rules, a player who grounds his club in a *hazard* will be assessed two penalty strokes. Johnson was seen on the television replay grounding his club not once, but twice before hitting his second shot.

Upon finishing the hole with a bogey, and a final round of 71, Johnson was notified that a penalty had been officially declared. The two-stroke infraction cost him not only the outright championship, but even a chance to participate in a playoff with Bubba Watson and Martin Kaymer, who eventually won the tournament. It was a painful lesson for the PGA's rising star. He was so close to victory, yet so far away.

Martha and I thoroughly enjoyed our visit to Wisconsin. After arriving at a Chicago airport, we rented a car, drove 140 miles north on the Interstate, sailed through the heart of Milwaukee, and found our way to Kohler. The only thing we had known about this quaint community before our trip was that they were known for their chocolates and for making a reputable line of toilets. Our appreciation for Kohler, the town, has grown considerably since then.

After spending the night at the five-star American Club Resort Hotel, Martha and I made the twenty-minute drive north to Whistling Straits, anticipating a morning round on its signature course. We presented our voucher at the pro shop and were assigned a caddy who would handle both sets of our clubs. No golf carts here. The Straits is a "walk only" course.

Our caddy was an affable young man who had emigrated from Cuba. We exchanged pleasantries and thought of a dozen or more questions we might like to ask him. Not wanting to pry into his personal life, however, we held most of those thoughts to ourselves, hoping that by the end of the round he might become more open and share his story.

After confirming our starting time, the caddy directed us to the practice area where we hit our warm-up shots. A few short iron strikes, a swing or two with the driver and five-wood, and I was ready to go. Martha always takes the practice range more seriously than I do, so I waited a few minutes for her to finish before we headed for the first tee box.

There was something exhilarating about that morning. The breeze blowing from Lake Michigan was cool, but the sky was clear, and the sunshine was promising that this would be a good day to play golf. Adding to my excitement, both Martha and I had good drives on the first hole. The caddy smiled, gave us a nod of approval, and led us down the fairway. We were off!

At this point in the round, walking the course was a refreshing exercise. Unburdened from having to manage my own clubs, I turned to Martha and said that I felt like belting out a few bars from "Oh, What a Beautiful Mornin'." She pleaded that I not. So, I refrained, but thought to myself, *it does not get much better than this*. And, honestly, it did not.

Links golf may not be my game. During the front nine, I found every sand dune Pete Dye ever thought of placing on the course. The rough gobbled up my wayward shots as if they were candy corn. By the time we made the turn, I had begun to wonder if I had brought enough golf balls for eighteen holes. *Maybe the back nine will be easier.* It was not.

On the thirteenth hole, I found my well-struck fairway shot lying in one of the deepest pot bunkers on the course. My sand game has never been my friend, even in shallow bunkers. To hit out of this hazard required skills I only dreamed of having. After five unsuccessful cracks at hitting over the bunker's towering lip, I picked up my ball and threw it toward the green. Our caddy had seen such chicanery before. He was not amused.

As we came to the eighteenth tee box, I breathed a sigh of relief and utter exhaustion. Thankfully, the end was in sight. Before hitting my last drive, I asked the caddy if he knew the location of the infamous bunker that derailed Dustin Johnson's bid for the 2010 Wanamaker Trophy. He nodded and said he would show us the spot.

Trudging up a small hillside, we came to an area of shallow patches of grass and sand. It was easy to see why Johnson said he had no idea he was standing in a bunker. I tried to imagine his frustration of being so close to winning the championship yet having to go home in a tie for fifth. It reminded me of something I had heard years before.

A former university president was a dear friend and mentor. He had a favorite expression, "Don't mess up on the eighteenth green." Of course, he was not talking about *golf*. He was referring to *life*. That refrain has echoed in my ears often when approaching the completion of any assignment. *Finish strong! Do not allow victory to slip through your hands. Soldier on to the final step of the journey.*

Winners know how to finish what they start. As they say of the opera, "It's not over until the fat lady sings." A typical golf tournament includes four times around the eighteen-hole circuit—72 holes in all, each as important as the next. The winner's earnings are not awarded until the last putt is sunk.

No one doubts that Dustin Johnson has the mental toughness to compete at the PGA's highest level. He has won his share of tournaments, including some of the majors, and has nothing more to prove. But on a fateful day at Whistling Straits in 2010, victory proved to be illusive. He would like to have had one more crack at the finishing hole.

—

Great is the art of beginning, but greater is the art of ending" – **Henry Wadsworth Longfellow**

10

FOCUS ON WINNING

No, *winning is not everything*, but if you want to claim the trophy, the thought *what does it take to be a winner* must enter your mind. Those who make it to the top rarely get there by accident. They win because they focus on the outcome of each shot, or more importantly, on the outcome of each decision in life.

Where do I need this ball to land to be ready for my next shot? What is my best chance of making par, or less, on this hole? What will it take for me to win the tournament? Focus on the outcome. Focus on winning!

John Byron Nelson, Jr. was a winner! He was a champion on the golf course, and he was a role model for human decency in every aspect of his life. Nelson's peers called him, "Lord Byron." Ken Venturi, a fellow golfer and broadcasting colleague, may have described Nelson best when he said, "His legacy is that you can argue over who is the greatest golfer who has ever lived, but he [Nelson] is the finest gentleman who ever played the game of golf."

A few months before Nelson died in 2006, I had the pleasure of meeting with him and his wife Peggy at their home in Roanoke, Texas. A mutual friend had asked Nelson if he would write the foreword to my book, *Fairways and Green Pastures*, and he had agreed to do so. The visit was an occasion for me to thank him personally and present him a copy of the finished product. He could not have been more gracious.

I wish I could tell you that I learned the secret of how to play great golf that evening and that my handicap dropped five strokes after the visit. But that is not what happened. In fact, the subject of golf barely surfaced in our conversation. He had played a few rounds at Horseshoe Bay and had good memories of his days on Ram Rock, the course that became the backcloth for *Fairways*.

We shared thoughts about our Christian faith and our mutual fellowship in the churches of Christ.

He was raised in that tradition and so was I. Looking back I think of the evening as a surreal moment in my life, an opportunity to be in the presence of greatness.

Byron Nelson was the consummate Southern gentleman. He was modest about his accomplishments, often resorting to self-effacing humor to lessen the regal aura that surrounded him. In his autobiography, *How I Played the Game*, Nelson humorously reflected upon his first year of marriage when his wife, Louise, chided him for buying five new drivers during the year while she had bought neither a new dress nor pair of shoes. She said, "[E]ither you don't know what kind of driver you want, or you don't know how to drive."

Few professional golfers have won more tournaments than Nelson. His 52 PGA victories, including five major championships, place him well within the top ten winners of all time. What is amazing about his record, however, is that he achieved most of those victories before the age of 34, when he retired from full-time competition to pursue cattle ranching in Texas. Nelson had his personal priorities clearly established in his mind and he knew how to bring balance into his life.

Nelson holds one PGA record that may never be eclipsed. In 1945, he won eighteen PGA events, eleven of them in a row. It was an incredible feat, one that never had occurred before and not likely to be broken in the near future. Arnold Palmer said of Nelson's remarkable year, "In 1945 Byron Nelson was the greatest golfer of all time. . . [He] was as close to a machine as anyone who ever played golf."

A few cynical sportswriters have taken exception to Palmer's assessment of Nelson, pointing out that his streak occurred during the last year of World War II when PGA ranks had been thinned due to professional golfers serving in the armed forces. That does not account, however, for the fact that Sam Snead and Ben Hogan, two of the greatest golfers of their generation, were actively playing in 1945. Snead won six tournaments and Hogan won five.

Jackie Burke, Jr., a contemporary of Nelson and a PGA Hall of Fame honoree, had an interesting way of looking at the critics' disparaging comments. "I don't care if he was playing against orangutans, winning eleven straight is amazing," Burke said.

Whenever asked to comment about the streak, Nelson suggested two focal points that kept propelling him to victory. First, he had a deep yearning to buy a ranch where he could raise cattle and he needed the tournament prize money to make the purchase. Each win brought him closer to his goal.

Second, he viewed the streak as an opportunity to set golfing records that would establish his place in annals of the sport. In the end, he did both. Nelson bought the cattle ranch, and his name is well established in the PGA record books.

Nelson left the professional golf circuit in 1946, but he stayed close to the game for the remainder of his life. In 1953 Nelson made a cameo appearance in *The Caddy*, a sports comedy starring Dean Martin and Jerry Lewis. He also produced a successful series of videotaped golf lessons.

During the 1960s and 1970s, he joined the ABC television crew, providing "color commentary" to the weekly broadcasts of PGA events. He was gone from the game, but not forgotten. Both the PGA Hall of Fame and the World Golf Hall of Fame inducted him into their elite circles of honorees.

When the United States Ryder Cup team was chosen in 1965, Nelson was named its non-playing captain. It was an assignment he took seriously, determined to lead the American team to victory. He was concerned, however, about the health of two players and was not surprised that the Americans were considered the underdogs.

Attending a press conference at Royal Birkdale Golf Club in Southport, England, the British captain, Harry Weetman, boasted of having the stronger team and predicted a British victory. Nelson, in his congenial manner responded to his rival, "Harry, we didn't come three thousand miles to lose." The Americans made good on his promise, defeating the Brits 19 and a half points to 12 and a half.

In 1968, the Dallas Open, an annual event on the PGA Tour, became known as the Byron Nelson Classic. It was the first time one of the tour stops had been named for a professional golfer. Martha and I were privileged to attend the Classic one year when it was being played at the TPC Four Seasons Course in Los Colinas, Texas. There was Nelson, seated near the eighteenth green, respect being paid to him by each competitor as he completed his round. No doubt about it: the man was a legend in his own lifetime.

So, what was it that made John Byron Nelson, Jr. such a winner? His physical and mental talents? His persistence? As with any successful person, it was combination of qualities, blended and baked into the whole. He was a man of dreams, guided by conscience and integrity, who knew how to focus on winning.

The best advice on winning comes from Lord

Byron himself. In an interview recounting highlights of his career, Nelson said:

> "Winners are different. They're a different breed of cat. I think the reason is, they have an inner drive and are willing to give of themselves whatever it takes to win. It's a discipline that a lot of people are not willing to impose upon themselves. It takes a lot of energy, a different way of thinking."

Who is a better subject to wrap up this treatise on winning than Lord Byron? He was, and still is the personification of a winner!

———

"The first requisite for success is to develop the ability to focus" – Thomas A. Edison

NOTES

Shell's Wonderful World of Golf by Golf Days (YouTube), 2015.

Nelson, Byron; Bradley, Jon. *How I Played the Game,* Dell Publishing, 1993.

Bradley, Jon. *Quotable Byron,* Towle House Publishing, 2002.

Barkow, Al. *Gettin' to the Dance Floor: An Oral History of American Golf,* Short Hills, New Jersey, Buford Books, 1986, p. 84.

Arnold Palmer Hauser, Thomas with Arnold Palmer. *Arnold Palmer: A Personal Journey,* San Francisco Collins Publishers, 1994, p. 26.

Bonk, Thomas. "Lord Byron," *Los Angeles Times,* March 11, 1995.

Barron, David. "Byron Nelson: 1912-2006," *Houston Chronicle,* Sept 27, 2006.

Other Books
Written by J. Terry Johnson

Jubilee: a colorful pictorial history of the first fifty years of Oklahoma Christian University. (2000)

Fairways and Green Pastures: A gift book with thoughts inspired by the eighteen holes of Ram Rock Golf Course at Horseshoe Bay Resort (foreword by PGA Hall of Fame honoree Byron Nelson; 2006)

Kirby: A paperback memoir of a state championship baseball team (foreword by former Attorney General John Ashcroft, 2008)

Cardinal Fever: A paperback memoir for St. Louis Cardinal baseball fans (foreword by MLB Hall of Fame honoree Whitey Herzog, 2009)

Awakenings: A paperback coming-of-age memoir (foreword by international recording artist Pat Boone, 2010)

Two Parts Sunshine: Biography and cookbook featuring Marty Johnson (foreword by OU women's basketball coach Sherri Coale, 2010)

10 Critical Factors in Fundraising: A book about raising financial support for nonprofits (Foreword by Pepperdine University president Andrew K. Benton, 2011)

Be of Good Cheer: A daily devotional book to encourage spiritual growth (2012)

Wounded Eagle: A novel about Major League Baseball in San Antonio (foreword by MLB Hall of Fame honoree Nolan Ryan, 2013)

A Glorious Church: A history of the New Testament Church (2015)

Walk in Love: Selected quotations from the author (2020)

My Animal Friends: A children's book about animals in the Texas Hill Country (2021)

10 Essential Thoughts for Winners: A book on what it takes to be a winner (foreword by PGA legend Loren Roberts, 2021)